Andrew Smith Hallidie

Cable Car Inventor

By Lisa Zamosky

Table of Contents

Chapter 1

Who Was Andrew Smith Hallidie?

In 1869, on a rainy summer day in San Francisco, Andrew Smith Hallidie *(HAL i dee)* saw a terrible accident.

In the decades of the 1800s people used horses to pull heavy streetcars up the hills of San Francisco. It often took four or five horses to do the job.

Horses were once used to pull streetcars through the active streets of San Francisco.

This is San Francisco in the 1800s. The city is famous for its steep hills.

On that day, Andrew Smith Hallidie watched five horses fall down a hill. They had slipped on the wet street. All five horses died. This did not violate the law during that time.

It was a terrible sight to everyone who saw it. But it gave Andrew Smith Hallidie, a mechanical genius, an idea for a great invention.

Andrew Smith Hallidie was born in London, England, on March 16, 1836. His mother was named Julia Johnston Smith. His father, also named Andrew Smith, was an engineer and inventor. His most important invention was the metal wire rope. In fact, he had the first patent in England for making wire rope.

Andrew Smith, the son, took the last name Hallidie to honor his uncle, Sir Andrew Hallidie.

⊙ Andrew Smith Hallidie grew up in London, England, in the 1830s.

⌢ Hallidie and his father traveled to the United States by ship.

At age 13, Hallidie began working in a machine shop. The skills he learned there helped him later in his life. At night he studied. Working during the day and studying at night affected his health. His father volunteered to take him to California.

They left England for America on a ship. It was a long journey. It took 15 days before they landed in New York.

After spending 16 days in New York, they journeyed to San Francisco.

Hallidie and his father arrived in California during the Gold Rush. People from all over the world were coming to California to find gold and get rich. Andrew Hallidie's father had the same hope for himself.

◔ Men mined for gold at a California gold mine.

Father and son first went to the gold mines in Mariposa *(mah ree POH suh)* County. But Andrew Smith Senior did not earn as much money there as he had hoped. He decided to return to England. Andrew Smith had stayed in California for just one year. But young Hallidie stayed in California. He was only 17 years old.

⋔ Miners crowded the fields looking for gold.

During the next years, Andrew Hallidie did all kinds of work. He fixed tools and built bridges. He worked on ditches, roads, and trails. He also mined.

Like everyone else, he hoped to get rich during the Gold Rush. But times were tough. He had some luck finding gold, but he never found enough. Money was very tight. Some days, he barely had enough to eat.

Chapter 2

Using Wire Rope

For several years, Hallidie moved from one mining camp to the next. He kept hoping for a change in his luck. He also continued to study.

In 1855, at the age of only 19, he built a wire suspension bridge across Sacramento's American River. He did this using his father's metal wire rope technology.

⏻ This bridge is similar to the one Andrew Hallidie built in 1855.

Hallidie next worked at a mine at the American River. The mine was on a hillside, high above a mill. Mining cars were moved to and from the mill below with rope.

But the rope began to wear out after only a little more than one month. Hallidie built a thick wire rope instead. It was so strong it lasted for two years.

⟳ Hallidie's wire rope was used in both mines and California's gold fields.

⌕ Hallidie was president of California Wire Works in San Francisco.

Hallidie moved to San Francisco and started his own company. The company produced wire rope. He also continued to build bridges.

Hallidie became very famous as a suspension bridge builder. But the work of building bridges was very hard. It kept him away from San Francisco for long periods of time.

Chapter 3

The Cable Car Comes to Life

Over the next several years, Hallidie patented many of his inventions. One invention was the Hallidie Ropeway. This was a way to move supplies across places with many mountains.

Hallidie was worried about the strength of the cable used to move the supplies. So he developed a steel cable that was much stronger and did not break.

↻ This is Hallidie's patent for his wire rope and cable invention.

Hallidie had already built many ropeways. Now he had an idea that he hoped would stop streetcar accidents in San Francisco. He thought that streetcars could be pulled with cables instead of horses.

Hallidie went to work on his idea. His plan was for an underground cable that would be attached to the streetcars. A machine would pull the cable and the streetcar would move.

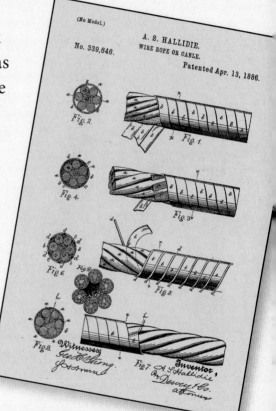

⋂ Detailed pictures of Hallidie's wire cable

He had the plan. Now Hallidie needed money. He found men who were willing to give him money to build his cable cars.

At five o'clock in the morning on August 1, 1873, the first cable car was tested. Hallidie and his business partners stood at an intersection. The cable car ran just as planned. It was a success!

⌒ The man seated at the front of the streetcar, on the left side, might be Andrew Smith Hallidie.

Hallidie's hard work transformed travel. Cities all over the country built cable railroads using Hallidie's invention. This made him a rich man.

On April 24, 1900, Andrew Hallidie died in San Francisco. Today, many people travel to the city just to ride Hallidie's cable cars.

On the spot where Clay and Kearny streets meet in San Francisco, there is a plaque honoring Andrew Smith Hallidie. It is here that the first cable car ride took place.

Comprehension Check

Summarize

Use a chart to record information from the text and what you know. Then make generalizations. Use the generalizations to summarize the text.

Information from Text	What I know	Generalization

Think and Compare

1. Reread pages 9–11. What generalization can you make from the information? *(Make Generalizations)*

2. Cable cars are important to the people of California. Tell about something that is important where you live. *(Apply)*

3. Cable cars are popular today. Why might people visiting California want to ride them? *(Evaluate)*